A Note to Parents

DK READERS is a compelling program for beginning readers, designed in conjunction with leading literacy experts, including Dr. Linda Gambrell, Distinguished Professor of Education at Clemson University. Dr. Gambrell has served as President of the National Reading Conference and the College Reading Association, and as President of the International Reading Association.

Beautiful illustrations and superb full-color photographs combine with engaging, easy-to-read stories to offer a fresh approach to each subject in the series. Each DK READER is guaranteed to capture a child's interest while developing his or her reading skills, general knowledge, and love of reading.

The five levels of DK READERS are aimed at different reading abilities, enabling you to choose the books that are exactly right for your child:

Pre-level 1: Learning to read
Level 1: Beginning to read
Level 2: Beginning to read alone
Level 3: Reading alone
Level 4: Proficient readers

The "normal" age at which a child begins to read can be anywhere from three to eight years old. Adult participation through the lower levels is very helpful for providing encouragement, discussing storylines, and sounding out unfamiliar words.

No matter which level you select, you can be sure that you are helping your child learn to read, then read to learn!

LONDON, NEW YORK, MUNICH,
MELBOURNE, AND DELHI

Series Editor Deborah Lock
U.S. Editor John Searcy
Art Editor Mary Sandberg
Production Editor Siu Chan
Production Pip Tinsley
Jacket Designer Mary Sandberg
Photographer Simon Rawles

Reading Consultant
Linda Gambrell, Ph.D.

First American Edition, 2008
08 09 10 11 12 10 9 8 7 6 5 4 3 2 1
Published in the United States by DK Publishing
375 Hudson Street, New York, New York 10014

DK books are available at special discounts when purchased in bulk for
sales promotions, premiums, fund-raising, or educational use.
For details, contact:
DK Publishing Special Markets
375 Hudson Street
New York, New York 10014
SpecialSales@dk.com

A catalog record for this book is available
from the Library of Congress.

ISBN: 978-0-7566-3458-2 (Paperback)
ISBN: 978-0-7566-3459-9 (Hardcover)

Color reproduction by Colourscan, Singapore
Printed and bound in China by L. Rex Printing Co. Ltd.

The publisher would like to thank Islington Football Development
Partnership for the use of the sports ground and Team Colours Ltd.
for part of the strip. Also thanks to Poppy Joslin for her assistance.

Models: Alex Webb, George Webb, Thomas Webb,
Charlie Adair-Hedges, Aymen Azaze, Shakur Cover, Ollie Francis,
Freya Hann, Rosie Nirawan, Michael Okello, Faye Perkins,
and the coach, Oliver Beccles.

All other images © Dorling Kindersley
For further information see: www.dkimages.com

Discover more at
www.dk.com

DK READERS

BEGINNING **1** TO READ

Let's Play Soccer

Written by Patricia J. Murphy

DK Publishing

Today was Erik's first day
at soccer practice.
Erik put on his soccer shoes.
He strapped his shin guards
to his lower legs.
He pulled his socks over
his shin guards.

Erik was ready for
soccer practice
to begin!

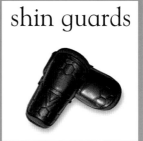

shin guards

"Welcome," said Coach Smith
to the players.
"Together, you'll learn how
to play soccer."
He told them three rules.
"Play your best, play fair, and
play without using your hands or
arms—unless you are the goalie!"

goalie

"First, we have to warm up,"
said Coach Smith.
"This will get our muscles ready!"
Everyone did jumping jacks.
Erik jumped with his legs and
arms apart, and then together.

Afterward, they all
jogged in place.

muscle

Next, Coach Smith led the team in stretches.

"Stretching will help keep us from getting hurt!" he said. "Hold each stretch for ten seconds."

"My muscles feel ready,"
said Erik.

"Good!" said Coach Smith.

"Then it's time to learn some
soccer skills."

"Passing means kicking the ball to another player on your team," said Coach Smith.

"It's the best way to move the ball to the goal.

You have to kick with the inside or the outside of your foot."

Erik, Beth, and Henry passed
the ball to one another.
"Good passes, everyone!"
said Coach Smith.

"In a game, you should only pass to a player who is free to take the ball."

"Let's try running with the ball,"
said Coach Smith.
"This is called dribbling."
Coach Smith dribbled
around some cones.

"To dribble, you have to move the ball with the tops of your feet," said Coach Smith. "Now, you try!"

Erik started dribbling around
the cones.
"Keep your head up," said
Coach Smith, "so you can see
both the ball and the field."
Erik tried looking up
and dribbling.
"Dribbling is hard work!" he said.

cones

"Let's shoot some goals,"
said Coach Smith.
The players kicked the ball
at the goal one by one.
Erik tried and missed.

"Keep your eye on the ball and aim for a corner of the goal," said Coach Smith. Erik tried again and scored!

goal

"Remember," said Coach Smith,
"the team that scores
the most goals wins!
But it's more important
to try your best and have fun."

"Let's take a water break.
Then, we'll play a game
of soccer,"
said Coach Smith.
He split the group
into two teams.

whistle

Coach Smith blew a whistle
to start the game.
Henry kicked the ball
from the center of the field,
and passed it to Erik.

Erik dribbled the ball
and passed it to Beth.
Beth kicked the ball
into the goal.
"Super teamwork!"
said Coach Smith.

"The score is 1-0," said Coach Smith, "and it's the yellow team's turn to kick off."

The game went on.
The players passed and dribbled
the ball up and down the field.

Coach Smith blew a long whistle
to end the game.
Erik's team cheered.
They had won!

Everyone shook hands.
"Good game!" said Erik
to the players on the yellow team.

Coach Smith talked about
the game while the players
cooled down.

"Are there any questions?"
asked Coach Smith.

"When's our next practice?"
asked Erik.

"Next week," said Coach Smith.
"Until then, remember
to practice your skills at home."

Glossary

 Goal a net that players try to get the ball into

 Goalie a player who tries to keep the ball out of the goal

 Muscle a body part under your skin that makes you move

 Shin guards pads that protect your lower legs

 Whistle a loud instrument used to start and stop a game